Hymns for mostly manuals

Hymns for mostly manuals

arranged by Colin Hand

Kevin Mayhew

We hope you enjoy the music in this book. Further copies are available
from your local music shop or Christian bookshop.

In case of difficulty, please contact the publisher direct by writing to:

The Sales Department
KEVIN MAYHEW LTD
Rattlesden
Bury St Edmunds
Suffolk
IP30 0SZ

Phone 01449 737978
Fax 01449 737834
E-mail info@kevinmayhew.com

Please ask for our complete catalogue of outstanding Church Music.

First published in Great Britain in 1998 by Kevin Mayhew Ltd.

ISBN 1 84003 161 1
ISMN M 57004 071 1
Catalogue No: 1400170

0 1 2 3 4 5 6 7 8 9

Front Cover: *Prisoners of Conscience* (detail) – stained glass window in Salisbury Cathedral.
Photograph by Derek Forss. Reproduced by kind permission.
Cover design by Jaquetta Sergeant.

Music Editor: Donald Thomson
Music setting by Lynwen Davies

Printed and bound in Great Britain by
Caligraving Limited Thetford Norfolk

Foreword

This collection of two hundred favourite hymn tunes has been provided with easy, supportive organ pedal parts and is directed towards the many pianists who regularly lead the singing at their local church services, playing the organ manuals alone.

Several of the arrangements call for the use of only two pedals and most of the others use only three, two of which are adjacent notes. A handful use four pedals - two pairs of adjacent notes. This means that, once the player's feet have been positioned over the appropriate pedals at the onset of the hymn, they can remain there for its duration.

Organ music is usually written on three staves, but in a two-stave layout as here, the bass line of the four part harmony is played on the pedals. Present-day pedal technique is based upon the use of both toe and heel of each foot:

∨	Right toe
⊙	Right heel
∧	Left toe
⊽	Left heel

In playing, the pedal notes should be depressed by movement from the ankle rather than the knee.

The written compass of the pedal board extends from 𝄢 upwards for about two and a half octaves to F or G.

Before starting the hymn, a glance along the bass line will show which pedal notes are required. The feet should then be positioned over the appropriate notes in accordance with the symbols, and remain there for the duration of the hymn. For adjacent pairs of notes, the foot should be turned so that the toe and heel are each over their respective notes. If one of them is a 'black' note the whole foot will need to be further forward than for the 'white' keys. One should try to avoid tying repeated pedal notes because repetition can assist rhythmic drive and help to give congregational singing a clear lead.

Since organs differ so widely, the choice of pedal stops must be left to the player. Some small instruments may have only two pedal stops, e.g. 16' Bourdon and 8' Flute. In general practice, however, a 16' stop needs to be drawn for most hymns, and it is advisable to couple the pedals to the manual upon which the hands are playing by drawing the appropriately named stop – Great to Pedal, Swell to Pedal or (on three-manual organs) Choir to Pedal. This duplicates the pedal line on the manual.

COLIN HAND

Contents

	Hymn No.		Hymn No.
He's got whe whole world	70	Morning Light	106
Hollingside	71	Moscow	107
Holyrood	72	Mount Ephraim	108
Horsley	73	Narenza	109
Hyfrydol	74	Nativity	110
Innocents	75	Neander	111
Irish	76	Nicaea	112
Jackson	77	North Coates	113
Joy to the world (Antioch)	78	Nottingham	114
Kilmarnock	79	Nun danket	115
Kum ba yah	80	Ode to Joy	116
Lasst uns erfreuen	81	Old Hundredth	117
Laudate Dominum (Gauntlett)	82	*Old 134th*	168
Laudate Dominum (Parry)	83	Olivet	118
Laudes Domini	84	O Perfect Love	119
Laus Deo (Redhead No.46)	85	Oriel	120
Llanfair	86	O Waly Waly	121
Lobe den Herren	87	Paderborn	122
London New	88	Penlan	123
Love divine	89	Petra (Redhead No.76)	124
Lux Eoi	90	Picardy	125
Lydia	91	Praise, my soul	126
Maccabaeus	92	Quam dilecta	127
Mannheim	93	Quem pastores	128
Margaret	94	Ravenshaw	129
Martyrdom	95	*Redhead No. 46*	85
Melcombe	96	*Redhead No.76*	124
Melita	97	Regent Square	130
Merton	98	Repton	131
Miles Lane	99	Rhuddlan	132
Misericordia	100	Richmond	133
Monkland	101	Rievaulx	134
Monks Gate	102	Rockingham	135
Monmouth	103	Royal Oak	136
Montgomery	104	Sagina	137
Morning Hymn	105	Salzburg	138

1 ABENDS

Herbert Stanley Oakeley (1830-1903)

2 ABERYSTWYTH

Joseph Parry (1841-1903)

3 ABRIDGE

Isaac Smith (1734-1805)

4 ALBANO

Vincent Novello (1781-1861)

5 ALLELUIA DULCE CARMEN (TANTUM ERGO)

Melody from 'Essay on the Church Plain Chant' (1782)

6 ALL SAINTS

Adapted by William Henry Monk (1823-1889)
from 'Geistreiches Gesangbuch', Darmstadt (1698)

7 AMAZING GRACE

American Folk Melody

8 ANGEL VOICES

Edwin George Monk (1819-1900)

9 ANGELUS

Adapted from a melody by George Joseph
in Scheffler's 'Heilige Seelenlust', Breslau (1657)

10 AR HYD Y NOS

Traditional Welsh Melody

11 AURELIA

Samuel Sebastian Wesley (1810-1876)

12 AUSTRIA

Croatian folk melody adapted by Franz Joseph Haydn (1732-1809)

17

13 BATTLE HYMN

Traditional American Melody

14 BELMONT

Adapted from William Gardiner's 'Sacred Melodies' (1812)

15 BISHOPTHORPE

Jeremiah Clarke (c.1674-1707)

16 BLAENWERN

William Penfro Rowlands (1860-1937)

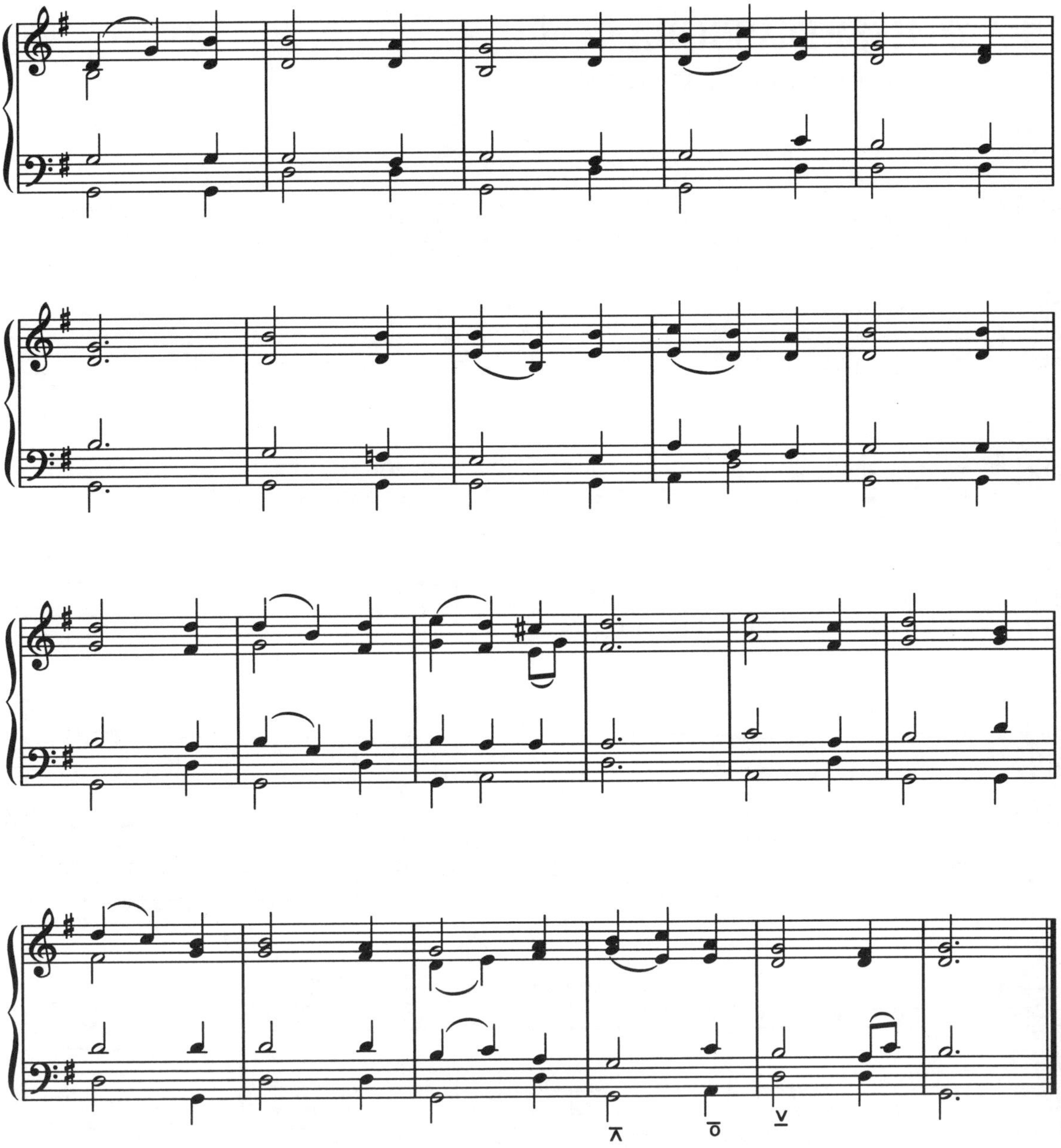

17 BLESSED ASSURANCE

Phoebe Palmer Knapp (1839-1908)

18 BRESLAU

Melody from 'As Hymnodus Sacer' (1625)

19 BRISTOL

Thomas Ravenscroft (c.1582-c.1633)

20 BUCKLAND

Leighton George Hayne (1836-1883)

21 BULLINGER

Ethelbert William Bullinger (1837-1913)

24

22 BUNESSAN

Traditional Gaelic Melody

23 BYZANTIUM

Thomas Jackson (1715-1781)

24 CAITHNESS

Melody from 'Scottish Psalter' (1635)

25 CAPEL

Traditional English carol collected by Lucy Broadwood (1858-1929)

26 CAPETOWN

Friedrich Filitz (1804-1876)

27 CARLISLE

Charles Lockhart (1745-1815)

28 CASWALL

Friedrich Filitz (1804-1876)

29 CELESTE

Melody from 'Lancashire Sunday School Songs' (1857)

30 CHARITY

John Stainer (1840-1901)

31 CHILDHOOD

University of Wales (1923)

32 CRIMOND

Jessie Seymour Irvine (1836-1887)

33 CROSS OF JESUS

John Stainer (1840-1901)

34 CRÜGER

From a melody in the 'Gesangbuch' of Johann Crüger (1598-1662)

35 CULBACH

Melody from Johann Scheffler's 'Heilige Seelenlust' (1657)

36 CWM RHONDDA

John Hughes (1873-1932)

37 DARWALL'S 148TH

John Darwall (1731-1789)

38 DAY OF REST

James William Elliott (1833-1915)

39 DEERHURST

James Langran (1835-1909)

40 DIADEM

James Ellor (1819-1899)

41 DIADEMATA

George Job Elvey (1816-1893)

42 DIX

Conrad Kocher (1786-1872) adapted by William Henry Monk (1823-1889)

43 DOMINUS REGIT ME

John Bacchus Dykes (1823-1876)

44 DONCASTER

Samuel Wesley (1766-1837)

45 DUKE STREET

Melody attributed to John Hatton (d.1793)

46 DUNDEE

Melody from 'Scottish Psalter' (1635)

47 DUNFERMLINE

Melody from 'Scottish Psalter' (1635)

48 EASTER HYMN

Adapted from a melody in 'Lyra Davidica' (1708)

49 EIN' FESTE BURG

Martin Luther (1483-1546)

50 ELLACOMBE

Melody from the 'Württemberg Gesangbuch' (1784)

51 EUDOXIA

Sabine Baring-Gould (1834-1924)

52 EVELYNS

William Henry Monk (1823-1889)

53 EVENTIDE

William Henry Monk (1823-1889)

54 EWING

Alexander Ewing (1830-1895)

55 FRANCONIA

Melody from 'Harmonischer Liederschatz' (1738)

56 GALILEE

Philip Armes (1836-1908)

57 GERONTIUS

John Bacchus Dykes (1823-1876)

58 GETHSEMANE

Philipp Bliss (1838-1876)

59 GOPSAL

George Frideric Handel (1685-1759)

60 GO, TELL IT ON THE MOUNTAIN

Traditional Melody

61 GWALCHMAI

John David Jones (1827-1870)

62 HALTON HOLGATE

Version of a melody by William Boyce (1711-1779)
in Samuel Sebastian Wesley's 'European Psalmist' (1872)

63 HANOVER

William Croft (1678-1727)

64 HAREWOOD

Samuel Sebastian Wesley (1810-1876)

65 HARLAN

Lowell Mason (1792-1872)

66 HEATHLANDS

Henry Smart (1813-1879)

67 HELMSLEY

From John Wesley's 'Select Hymns with Tunes Annext' (1765)

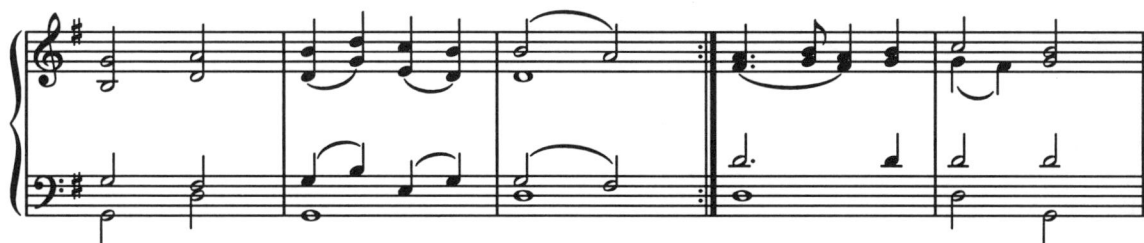

68 HEREFORD

Samuel Sebastian Wesley (1810-1876)

69 HERONGATE

Traditional English Melody

70 HE'S GOT THE WHOLE WORLD

Traditional Melody

71 HOLLINGSIDE

John Bacchus Dykes (1823-1876)

72 HOLYROOD

James Watson (1816-1880)

73 HORSLEY

William Horsley (1774-1858)

74 HYFRYDOL

Rowland Huw Pritchard (1811-1887)

75 INNOCENTS

'The Parish Choir' (1850)

76 IRISH

Melody from 'Hymns & Sacred Poems', Dublin (1749)

77 JACKSON

Thomas Jackson (1715-1781)

78 JOY TO THE WORLD (ANTIOCH)

George Frideric Handel (1685-1759)

79 KILMARNOCK

Neil Dougall (1776-1862)

80 KUM BAYAH

Spiritual

81 LASST UNS ERFREUEN

Melody from 'Geistliche Kirchengesang', Cologne (1623)

82 LAUDATE DOMINUM (Gauntlett)

Henry John Gauntlett (1805-1876)

83 LAUDATE DOMINUM (Parry)

Charles Hubert Hastings Parry (1848-1918)

84 LAUDES DOMINI

Joseph Barnby (1838-1896)

85 LAUS DEO (REDHEAD No. 46)

Richard Redhead (1820-1901)

86 LLANFAIR

Robert Williams (1781-1821)

87 LOBE DEN HERREN

Melody from 'Praxis Pietatis Melica' (1668)

88 LONDON NEW

'Scottish Psalter' (1635) adapted by John Playford

89 LOVE DIVINE

John Stainer (1840-1901)

90 LUX EOI

Arthur Seymour Sullivan (1842-1900)

91 LYDIA

Thomas Phillips (1735-1807)

92 MACCABAEUS

George Frideric Handel (1685-1759)

93 MANNHEIM

Friedrich Filitz (1804-1876)

94 MARGARET

Timothy Richard Matthews (1826-1910)

95 MARTYRDOM

Melody by Hugh Wilson (1766-1824)

96 MELCOMBE

Samuel Webbe (1740-1816)

97 MELITA

John Bacchus Dykes (1823-1876)

98 MERTON

William Henry Monk (1823-1889)

99 MILES LANE

William Shrubsole (1760-1806)

100 MISERICORDIA

Henry Smart (1813-1879)

101 MONKLAND

'Hymn Tunes of the United Brethren' (1824)
adapted by John Wilkes (1785-1869)

102 MONKS GATE

Traditional English Melody

103 MONMOUTH

Gabriel Davis (c.1768-1824)

104 MONTGOMERY

'Magdalen Hospital Hymns' (c.1760)

105 MORNING HYMN

François Hippolyte Barthélémon (1741 - 1808)

106 MORNING LIGHT

George James Webb (1803-1887)

107 MOSCOW

Melody from Madan's 'Collection' (1769)
adapted by Felice de Giardini (1716 -1796)

108 MOUNT EPHRAIM

Benjamin Milgrove (1731-1810)

109 NARENZA

Melody from Leisentritt's 'Catholicum Hymnologium Germanicum' (1584)
adapted by William Henry Havergal (1793-1870)

110 NATIVITY

Henry Lahee (1826-1912)

111 NEANDER

Melody by Joachim Neander (1640-1680)

112 NICAEA

John Bacchus Dykes (1823-1876)

113 NORTH COATES

Timothy Richard Matthews (1826-1910)

114 NOTTINGHAM

Wolfgang Amadeus Mozart (1756-1791) adapt.

115 NUN DANKET

Johann Crüger (1598-1662)

116 ODE TO JOY

Ludwig van Beethoven (1770-1827)

117 OLD HUNDREDTH

From the 'Genevan Psalter' (1551)

118 OLIVET

Lowell Mason (1792-1872)

119 O PERFECT LOVE

Jospeh Barnby (1838-1896)

120 ORIEL

From Caspar Ett's 'Cantica Sacra' (1840)

121 O WALY WALY

Somerset folk song collected by Cecil Sharpe (1859-1924)

122 PADERBORN

'Paderborn Gesangbuch' (1765)

123 PENLAN

David Jenkins (1848-1915)

124 PETRA (REDHEAD No.76)

Richard Redhead (1820-1901)

125 PICARDY

Traditional French Melody

126 PRAISE, MY SOUL

John Goss (1800-1880)

127 QUAM DILECTA

Henry Lascelles Jenner (1820-1898)

128 QUEM PASTORES

German Carol Melody (14th Century)

129 RAVENSHAW

Medieval German melody adapted by William Henry Monk (1823-1889)

130 REGENT SQUARE

Henry Smart (1813-1879)

131 REPTON

Charles Hubert Hastings Parry (1848-1918)

132 RHUDDLAN

Traditional Welsh melody from 'Musical Relicks of Welsh Bards' (1800)

133 RICHMOND

Melody adapted from Thomas Haweis (1734-1820)

134 RIEVAULX

John Bacchus Dykes (1823-1876)

135 ROCKINGHAM

Melody adapted by Edward Miller (1735-1807)

136 ROYAL OAK

Traditional English Melody

Fine

D.C.

137 SAGINA

Thomas Campbell (1825-1876)

138 SALZBURG

Jacob Hintze (1622-1702)

139 SANDON

Charles Henry Purday (1799-1885)

140 SANDYS

Traditional English carol from William Sandys' 'Christmas Carols' (1833)

141 SAVANNAH
John Wesley's 'Foundery Collection' (1742)

142 SHIPSTON
Warwickshire Ballad

143 SIMPLICITY

Orlando Gibbons (1583-1625)

144 SING HOSANNA

Traditional Melody

145 SLANE

Traditional Irish Melody

146 SOLOMON

Melody adapted from an aria in Handel's 'Solomon', (1749)

147 SONG 34 (ANGELS' SONG)

Orlando Gibbons (1583-1625)

148 SOUTHWELL (DAMON)

Adapted by William Damon (1540-1591)
from 'The Psalms in English Metre' (1579)

149 ST AGNES (Dykes)

John Bacchus Dykes (1823-1876)

150 ST ALBINUS

Henry John Gauntlet (1805-1876)

151 ST ALPHEGE

Henry John Gauntlett (1805-1876)

152 ST ANNE
William Croft (1678-1727)

153 ST BEES
John Bacchus Dykes (1823-1876)

154 ST BERNARD

Adapted from a melody in 'Tochter Sion' (1741)

155 ST CATHERINE

Samuel Flood Jones (1826-1895)

156 ST CECILIA

Leighton George Hayne (1836-1883)

157 ST CLEMENT

Clement Cotterill Scholefield (1839-1904)

158 ST COLUMBA

Irish melody (Petrie Collection)

159 ST CUTHBERT

John Bacchus Dykes (1823-1876)

160 ST DENIO

Traditional Welsh hymn melody from
John Robert's 'Caniadau y Cyssegre' (1839)

161 ST ETHELWALD
William Henry Monk (1823-1889)

162 ST FULBERT
Henry John Gauntlett (1805-1876)

Last verse

Al - le - lu - ia. A - men.

163 ST GEORGE'S WINDSOR

George Job Elvey (1816-1893)

164 ST GERTUDE

Arthur Seymour Sullivan (1842-1900)

165 ST HELEN

George Clement Martin (1844-1916)

166 ST HUGH

Edward John Hopkins (1818-1901)

167 ST MAGNUS

Jeremiah Clarke (c.1674-1707)

168 ST MICHAEL (OLD 134TH)

Melody adapted from 'Anglo-Genevan Psalms' (1561)

169 ST OSWALD

John Bacchus Dykes (1823-1876)

170 ST PETER

Alexander Robert Reinagle (1799-1877)

171 ST STEPHEN
William Jones (1726-1800)

172 ST THEODULPH
Melchior Teschner (1584-1635)

173 STEPHANOS

Henry Williams Baker (1821-1877)

174 STOCKTON

Thomas Wright (1763-1829)

175 STRACATHRO

Charles Hutcheson (1792-1860)

176 STRENGTH AND STAY

John Bacchus Dykes (1823-1876)

177 STUTTGART

German melody arranged by Christian Friedrich Witt (c. 1660-1716)

178 SURREY

Henry Carey (c.1690-1743)

179 SUSSEX

Traditional English melody

180 TALLIS'S CANON

Thomas Tallis (c.1505-1585)

181 TALLIS'S ORDINAL

Thomas Tallis (c.1505-1585)

182 THIS JOYFUL EASTERTIDE (VREUCHTEN)

17th Century Dutch melody

183 TO GOD BE THE GLORY

William Howard Doane (1823-1916)

184 TRURO

Melody from Thomas Williams's 'Psalmodia Evangelica' (1789)

185 TRUST AND OBEY

Daniel Brink Towner (1833-1896)

Refrain

186 UNIVERSITY
Charles Collignon (1725-1785)

187 UNIVERSITY COLLEGE
Henry John Gauntlett (1805-1876)

188 VENI EMMANUEL

Melody from a French Missal, adapted by Thomas Helmore (1811-1890)

* G♯ on last verse only

189 VICTORY

Giovanni Pierluigi da Palestrina (c.1525-1594)
adapted by William Henry Monk (1823-1889)

190 VULPIUS

Melchior Vulpius (c. 1560-1615)

191 WAREHAM

William Knapp (1698-1768)

192 WAS LEBET

Melody from the 'Rheinhardt MS', Üttingen (1754)

193 WESTMINSTER

James Turle (1802-1882)

194 WESTMINSTER ABBEY

Henry Purcell (1659-1695)

195 WHAT A FRIEND

Charles Crozat Converse (1832-1918)

196 WILL YOUR ANCHOR HOLD

Priscilla Jane Owens (1829-1899)

197 WILTSHIRE

George Thomas Smart (1776-1867)

198 WINCHESTER NEW

Melody from 'Musikalisches Handbuch', Hamburg (1690)

199 WIR PFLÜGEN

Johann Abraham Peter Schulz (1747-1800)

200 WÜRTTEMBURG

Melody from 'Hundert Arien', Dresden, (1694)

C/5